CANADA AT WAR

Dylan Kirk

Weigl

CALGARY
www.weigl.com

We acknowledge the financial support of the Government of Canada through the Book Publishing Industry Development Program (BPIDP) for our publishing activities.

Published by Weigl Educational Publishers Limited
6325 – 10 Street SE
Calgary, Alberta, Canada
T2H 2Z9

Web site: www.weigl.com

National Library of Canada Cataloguing-in-Publication Data

Kirk, Dylan
  Canada at war / Dylan Kirk.

  (Canadian history)
  Includes bibliographical references and index.
  ISBN 1-55388-016-1

  1. World War, 1914-1918--Canada. 2. World War, 1939-1945--Canada. 3. Canada--History--1914-1945. I. Title. II. Series: Canadian history (Calgary, Alta.)
  FC543.K57 2003   971.06   C2003-910135-5
  F1034.K57 2003

Printed in the United States of America
1 2 3 4 5 6 7 8 9 0   07 06 05 04 03

Project Coordinator
Heather C. Hudak
Substantive Editor
Donald Wells
Photo Researchers
Wendy Cosh
Pamela Wilton
Designer
Warren Clark
Layout
Bryan Pezzi
Katherine Phillips

Credits
Every reasonable effort has been made to trace ownership and to obtain permission to reprint copyright material. The publishers would be pleased to have any errors or omissions brought to their attention so that they may be corrected in subsequent printings.

Cover: Pilots with planes **(National Film Board of Canada/Canada Dept. of National Defence/National Archives of Canada PA-136047)**, CWACs **(Ken Bell/Canada Dept. of National Defence/National Archives of Canada PA-132838)**, Vimy Memorial **(Heather C. Hudak); Canadian Jewish Congress National Archives:** page 25R; **Glenbow Archives:** pages 11 (NA-1870-6), 22 (NC-6-11729), 23 (NA-2629-13); **Heather C. Hudak:** page 19; **Hulton|Archive by Getty Images:** pages 4, 5; **Courtesy Dave MacEwen:** page 43; **Courtesy Sandra MacEwen:** page 41; **National Archives of Canada:** pages 1 (Sgt. Karen M. Hermiston/Canada Dept. of National Defence PA-128229), 3T (William Rider-Rider/Canada Dept. of National Defence PA-003265), 3M (Dupras & Colas C-000694), 3B (Bud Glunz PA-193007), 6 (C-095746), 8 (PA-107378), 9 (Canada Dept. of National Defence PA-004867), 10 (Canada Dept. of National Defence C-018734), 12 (W. I. Castle/Canada Dept. of National Defence PA-000848), 13 (Canada Dept. of National Defence PA-001371), 14 (Dupras & Colas C-000694), 15 (C-095730), 16 (William Rider-Rider/Canada Dept. of National Defence PA-003265), 17 (PA-122515), 20 (PA-025025), 21 (PA163001), 24 (C-029399), 25L (C-111012), 26 (C-022001), 27 (National Film Board of Canada/Canada Dept. of National Defence PA-136047), 28 (Heinrich Hoffman PA-164749), 30 (C-087137), 31 (Canada Dept. of National Defence PA-113249), 32 (Yousef Karsh PA-165806), 33 (Terry F. Rowe/Canada Dept. of National Defence PA-107934), 34 (National Film Board of Canada C-024452), 35 (Ken Bell/Canada Dept. of National Defence PA-132838), 36 (PA-802610), 37 (Donald I. Grant/Canada Dept. of National Defence PA-133930), 38 (Gilbert Alexander Milne/Canada Dept. of National Defence PA-137013), 39 (Alexander M. Stirton/Canada Dept. of National Defence PA-140417), 40 (Bud Glunz PA-193007); **Katherine Phillips:** page 7; **USHMM:** page 29.

CONTENTS

The EMPIRE and Europe

The desire for empire eventually led to World War I.

At the turn of the twentieth century, Canada was part of the British Empire. Other European nations wanted to create empires as well. This desire for empire led to World War I.

Germany, then called Prussia, was ruled by an emperor and a **chancellor**. The chancellor's name was Otto von Bismarck. He wanted to strengthen Germany's position in Europe rather than accumulate colonies around the world.

Germany was one of the most recent nations to join Europe's **Great Powers**. Austria-Hungary, France, Great Britain, and Russia were Europe's other Great Powers. Under Bismarck's guidance, Germany became an independent nation after winning three wars of unification in 1864, 1866, and 1870. Germany was able to gain power from France and Austria.

The Balance of Power

France and Russia agreed to defend one another if Germany attacked them. Knowing this, Bismarck maintained the European **balance of power** in order to prevent war. Great Britain also wanted Europe's balance of power to remain stable. Maintaining the balance of power kept continental Europe busy while Great Britain expanded its overseas empire.

Bismarck's reign as chancellor ended in 1890 with the rise of Emperor Wilhelm II. Wilhelm II envied Great Britain's overseas empire. Wilhelm II built a large navy. This allowed him to extend his power overseas and acquire overseas colonies. Great Britain responded by creating a huge naval building project of its own. The two nations competed to build the largest navy. This became known as the great Naval Arms Race of the 1890s. Great Britain built a larger navy than Germany, but it no longer trusted Wilhelm II.

■ Wilhelm II became the German emperor in 1888. His policies helped start World War I. When the German offensive failed in 1918, Wilhelm II was forced to abdicate his throne.

FURTHER UNDERSTANDING

Schlieffen Plan Germany planned to wage war against France and Russia many years before World War I. Alfred von Schlieffen, the German army's Chief of Staff, proposed a "win-hold-win" strategy. This meant Germany would attack and defeat France before Russia and Great Britain could respond. The German armies would quickly move back around to defeat Russia. Most of the German army would attack France, while the remaining few divisions would hold back Russia until France was defeated. Since France had strong defences on its border with Germany, the plan called for German troops to march through Belgium, Luxembourg, and Holland to get to Paris. Von Schlieffen thought these areas would be easier to pass through while Russia and Great Britain mobilized their armies in response to the attack. Helmuth von Moltke, the next German army Chief of Staff, modified the plan so that it did not include attacking Holland.

Historically, Great Britain and France did not have a good relationship. However, in 1905, Great Britain formed an *Entente Cordiale* with France and Russia in order to contain German expansion. They were known as the Triple Entente, and they were a great threat to Germany.

Austria-Hungary

At the beginning of the twentieth century, Austria-Hungary was a fading power in Europe. In order to maintain its position, Austria attempted to control former Yugoslavia, which is now the Balkan states of Bosnia, Herzegovina, and Serbia. Austria-Hungary was only able to take control of Bosnia and Herzegovina. Russia blocked Austria-Hungary's attempt to take over Serbia.

In 1909, Germany allied with Austria-Hungary to prevent Russian attack. This prevented war, but it brought together the rival nations and strengthened the alliance between France and Russia. These alliances created a dangerous situation in Europe, which eventually led to a world war.

In 1914, Austro-Hungarian Archduke Francis Ferdinand toured Bosnia and Herzegovina to mark the anniversary of the 1389 Battle of Kosovo. During this battle, Serbia was defeated by Ottoman Turks and lost the opportunity to become an empire. A Serbian member of the Black Hand terrorist group assassinated Ferdinand during the tour. Austria-Hungary declared war on Serbia on June 28, 1914, the same day Ferdinand was assassinated. Russia was obligated to defend Serbia and declared war on Austria-Hungary. In response, Germany declared war on Russia on August 1, and France on August 3. Following the Schlieffen Plan, Germany sent its armies through Belgium to Paris. Great Britain declared war on Germany for invading Belgium.

Most of the European powers did not expect a large European war, and they tried to stop it. However, it was too late. World War I had started.

■ Austro-Hungarian Archduke Francis Ferdinand became heir to the Austro-Hungarian crown after the deaths of his cousin, Prince Rudolph, in 1889, and of his father, in 1896.

CANADA Goes to War

Canada decided to support Great Britain in World War I as an independent nation and not as a colony.

Germany's invasion of Belgium forced Great Britain to declare war on Germany. As part of the British Empire, Canada was also at war. Although Canada had some **autonomy**, it supported Great Britain. Canadian Prime Minister Robert Borden offered assistance to Great Britain. Canada decided to support Great Britain in World War I as an independent nation and not as a colony.

Canada had a small army of about 3,000 troops, as well as the **militia**. There was a call for Canadian volunteers to fight. By October 1914, more than 30,000 Canadians were training under British instructors at Salisbury Plain in England. These soldiers formed the Canadian Expeditionary Force (CEF). They were deployed to France in the area of Ypres.

Young boys flocked to recruiting stations in Canada. Many thought the war would be an adventure; others dreamed of fighting for their country. The boys who enlisted did not really know what to expect.

Many people believed the war would end before Christmas, so those who did not enlist were considered cowards. To label a man as a coward for not enlisting, young women would hand white feathers to any man not wearing a uniform. This treatment made it difficult for the men who remained in Canada and worked in industry to support the war. To make people aware of their war efforts, special badges were worn by the men who served the nation at home.

FURTHER UNDERSTANDING

The Miracle on the Marne

At Mons, France, on August 23, 1914, the British Expeditionary Force (BEF), which had 70,000 troops, stood against the German First Army, which had 150,000 troops. The BEF inflicted heavy casualties on the Germans. However, the BEF was overrun because of its small number of troops. The BEF decided to fall back to the river Marne. The BEF and French Fifth and Sixth Armies stood together at the Marne on September 6. They attacked the German First Army. The British and French forces created a 50-kilometre gap between the German First Army and Second Army. The BEF and French armies rushed to push through the gap. During the 5-day battle, Paris taxicabs rushed 6,000 French troops to the front to relieve the French armies. This battle halted German progress toward Paris, but it failed to defeat the German armies.

Military terminology

There are several military terms that refer to groups of soldiers and how they are used in combat. The smallest organization is the section, which is made up of about 15 soldiers who are led by a non-commissioned officer. A platoon is made up of four sections (60 soldiers). A lieutenant leads the platoon. Four platoons make a company (240 soldiers and 6 officers). The company is usually led by a major. The battalion (1,000 soldiers and 36 officers), has four companies and is led by a lieutenant colonel. A division, which is led by a major-general, has three battalions. A corps, which is led by a lieutenant-general, has four divisions. One or two corps make up an army, which is commanded by a full general.

PUBLISHED BY THE ESSEX COUNTY RECRUITING COMMITTEE

■ Many enlistment posters were displayed throughout Canada at the beginning of the war. Communities wanted to send soldiers to fight, and healthy men felt pressured to enlist.

THE RACE TO THE SEA

The German army attacked Belgium on August 4, 1914. The Germans moved toward France, attempting to reach Paris. This would have removed France from the war, but because of the Miracle on the Marne, Paris was saved. However, there were still German armies in France. The Entente forces and the German armies attempted to **outflank** one another along the line from Switzerland to the English Channel. Along the front line, which was located in the area around Ypres at the English Channel ports, they dug trenches and erected barbed wire fortifications. If the Germans captured the ports, it would be difficult to get new troops from Great Britain to the European continent, and Germany would provide access to staging points for an assault on Great Britain. New Canadian recruits, inexperienced boys who had just arrived for battle, were placed in the most active sector of the Western Front—the Ypres **salient**. It was not long before they saw action.

The European Powers on August 4, 1914

- The "Central Powers"
- Countries that remained neutral on the outbreak of war, but later joined the Allied Powers
- Neutral States
- The "Entente" or "Allied Powers"

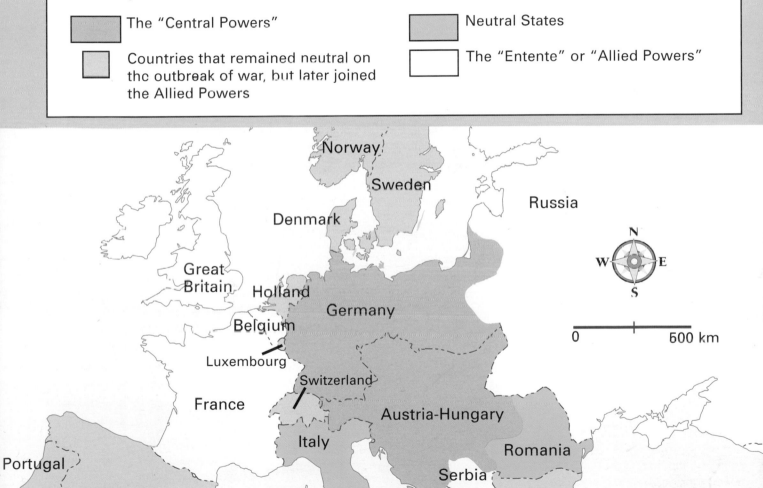

Canadians at YPRES

During the Second Battle of Ypres, Canadian troops were distinguished as determined soldiers.

Canadian troops stepped onto French soil for the first time as an army in December 1914. The first **regiment** posted to France was the Princess Patricia's Canadian Light Infantry. The remainder of the First Canadian Division was sent to France in February 1915, where they boarded trains and travelled to the fighting around the Ypres salient. The First Battle of Ypres had ended in November, but the Canadians were confronted with a terrible battle upon their arrival at Ypres.

The German army was developing a secret weapon: poison gas. It became one of the most feared weapons of World War I.

On April 22, 1915, French Algerian troops on the northern part of the Ypres salient saw a yellow-green cloud rise through the air. This cloud moved over the French Algerian trenches and soon entered the northwestern Canadian positions. Troops began choking and coughing up blood. Soon, German troops charged into the gas cloud's path. The French Algerians were driven

back, and the road to Ypres was left open for the German army to attack. Canadian troops were ordered to assist the French Algerians. The retreating French Algerians opened the Canadian left flank to attack, and the Germans rushed to attack the Canadian line.

While trying to stop the German advance, the Canadian line had to stretch out, creating gaps. The German penetration into the north face of the Ypres salient was very deep, and Belgian, Canadian, and French troops tried to shore up the defence. Even though the Canadian line needed support, the Canadian 10th and 16th Battalions counterattacked. On the night of April 22, 1915, they made a charge against German machine-gun nests. The 10th Battalion led the charge, and of the 816 men who marched off to battle, only 171 returned alive. Marshal Foch, the Allied supreme commander, commented that he thought this was the most amazing act of the Second Battle of Ypres. In their first battle, Canadian troops were distinguished as determined soldiers.

FURTHER UNDERSTANDING

The Ross rifle Canada had to choose a weapon to give its soldiers. One weapon was the British-made Lee-Enfield rifle, which had been designed in the 1890s. It was a simple and sturdy rifle that served the BEF well. The other weapon was the Ross rifle, a Canadian-made rifle that was very accurate. Buying it created jobs for Canadians. However, the Canadian government did not consider how the Ross rifle would react in wartime conditions. By 1915, soldiers lived and fought in trenches filled with mud and dirt. If mud or dirt got into the firing mechanism, the Ross rifle would stop working. Canadians tried to steal Lee-Enfield rifles whenever their Ross rifles stopped working.

■ Sir Charles Ross developed the Ross rifle as a military version of a Canadian-designed-and-built hunting rifle called the mannlicher.

THE FIRST GAS ATTACKS

In 1914, the French were the first to launch a gas attack. They fired tear gas grenades at the Germans. Though the grenades were ineffective, the attack encouraged the Germans to study and create a poisonous gas.

The first poisonous gas attacks were unsuccessful. The Germans developed a special **howitzer** shell that released sneezing powder when it exploded. This shell was tested on the British in October 1914. Apart from a few runny noses, the sneezing powder had no effect on the British troops. The Germans went on to develop more deadly gases. They decided that the release of chlorine by canister was the most effective way to suffocate large numbers of the enemy. Chlorine gas combines with water in the lungs, eyes, and nose to produce hydrochloric acid. This acid burns the skin and makes the lungs and nose bleed. It was not always fatal, but those who died usually choked to death on their own blood. Tested at the Second Battle of Ypres, Canadian soldiers and French Algerian troops were the first to experience a chlorine gas attack.

Soon, gas attacks were being launched by Allied troops as well. Gas masks became part of the standard army uniform, and they offered some protection against the deadly gas.

■ During the 48 hours the Canadian Army spent fighting at Ypres, 6,035 Canadian troops were killed.

The HOME FRONT

World War I forced the Canadian government to start acknowledging women's rights.

In Canada, thousands of young men left the work force to join the army. This created job opportunities across the nation. People flocked to fill these positions. Canada, which had many unemployed citizens, suddenly needed to fill 300,000 vacant jobs. Canada was asked to provide the British war effort with ammunition, grain, and meat. Farmers and private companies received large sums of cash to help meet demand. Meat exports increased from $6 million to $85 million. Other industries experienced a similar trend.

Early in the twentieth century, women were usually employed as teachers. When the war began and men enlisted to fight, vacancies opened in other industries. In order to accommodate the increased demand for exports, women were allowed to work in jobs that had been held by men.

The change in women's lifestyles brought changes in women's fashion. Women's dresses became more practical, and in some cases, their clothing started to resemble military uniforms. This was quite different from the long, narrow one-piece dresses worn earlier in the century.

Since women were now working outside the home, they started to demand social equality. For example, there was mounting pressure to grant women the right to vote. In 1916, women were allowed to vote in some provincial elections. The right to vote in federal elections was granted in 1918.

FURTHER UNDERSTANDING

National Research Council of Canada (NRC) The NRC was formed in 1916 as the Honourary Advisory Council for Scientific and Industrial Research. It funded research committees for special needs, offered science fellowships at Canadian universities, and carried out the first statistical review of Canada's scientific work force. An NRC national laboratory in Ottawa was authorized in 1928. War research included everything from medicine and food packaging to weapons and synthetic fuels.

■ More than 30,000 women worked in weapons factories during World War I. Thousands of women worked in banks, factories, farms, and offices.

In addition to working in jobs that were traditionally filled by men, women joined the army as nurses. They set up and operated nursing stations in the Balkans, Egypt, France, and Great Britain. The Canadian Medical Corps gave female nurses military rank. Of all the British forces, Canadian nurses were the only women granted this honour. World War I forced the Canadian government to start acknowledging women's rights.

Spurred by the need for new technologies for the war effort, the National Research Council of Canada (NRC) was formed in 1916. Acting as an advisory committee to the government, the NRC helped shape Canadian policy toward technology for the remainder of the war. The NRC still exists today, and is actively engaged in scientific research.

During the war, many Canadians worried about German nationals living in Canada. By 1915, there were public demands to prevent these people from promoting their loyalty to Germany. Some newspapers published **xenophobic**

articles. For example, John W. Dafoe commented in the *Winnipeg Free Press* that Canada should "clean the aliens out of this community and ship them back to their happy homes in Europe which vomited them forth a decade ago." Some companies fired foreign employees.

The government of Canada also worried that people without Canadian citizenship might act as spies. They forced non-Canadian residents into internment camps. Before the war was over, more than 8,500 people were placed in camps.

This was not the first time the Canadian government enacted xenophobic laws. In 1914, a group named the Asiatic Exclusion League fought to exclude people of East Asian descent from coming to Canada.

Although Canada was experiencing economic prosperity, there were many fears and problems. Women were still not considered full members of society. Non-Canadians were viewed with suspicion, and Canadian men were dying in a full-scale war in Europe.

■ More than 600 Ukrainians were interned under armed guard at the Castle Mountain internment camp in Alberta.

The SOMME Offensive

On July 1, 1916, Allied forces attacked on a broad front in the area of the Somme, France. The original plan was a full offensive, or mass attack, with mostly French troops, but the Germans attacked Verdun in an attempt to use **attrition** on the French army. The German attack was successful, and the British army had to carry out the Somme Offensive without the support of the French army. It was no longer a full-scale attack, but a diversion—an attack to take pressure off the French troops being attacked at Verdun.

The first day of the Somme Offensive is known as the worst day in the history of the British army. About 750,000 troops attacked after 8 days of heavy bombardment. At the end of the first attack, the British suffered 57,470 casualties. In total, the Allies suffered about 615,000 casualties, and 24,029 Canadian troops were killed in action. The Germans suffered about 650,000 casualties. The Somme Offensive lasted from July 1 to November 28, 1916. When it was over, the Allies had advanced 12 kilometres.

The Canadian Expeditionary Force (CEF) fought at the Somme and experienced some of the worst fighting of the war. The Newfoundland Regiment fought on the first day of fighting during the Battle of Beaumont Hamel. The regiment suffered 684 casualties, and 310 troops died. Only 68 Newfoundlanders remained uninjured after the fighting. When the CEF entered combat, the Battle of the Somme was already 2 months old. The Canadian forces took a long time to arrive in Somme because they were occupied by several attacks on the south end of the Ypres salient.

On September 15, 1916, the CEF attacked toward Courcelette, France. They were accompanied by the Entente's new military innovation—tanks. The Canadians had built a strong reputation at Ypres. After their actions at the Somme during the

FURTHER UNDERSTANDING

Attrition warfare Attrition warfare was the idea of German General Erich von Falkenhayn. He believed that the Germans should find a place on the French line where the French could not surrender. The Germans would attack this location with as much force as possible. Even if one German soldier died for every French soldier, the Germans would win the war because they had a larger population. The location chosen was Verdun. The purpose was not to win the battle, but to kill as many French soldiers as possible. The Somme Offensive slowed the attack at Verdun to a standstill, and General von Falkenhayn was replaced because his plan failed.

World War I tanks During World War I, the British invented and used the first working tank. The vehicles were named tanks because the British shipped them to battle in crates marked "tanks" in order to disguise them from the Germans. Tanks were first used on September 15, 1916, during the Battle of the Somme. The British used 49 tanks with disappointing results. Little more than one year later, however, in November 1917, 400 British tanks penetrated German lines near Cambrai and captured 8,000 German soldiers and 100 guns on the first day of the attack.

■ The howitzer was a type of cannon that had a short barrel. It was used to hit hidden, fixed targets. The howitzer was one of the weapons used to fight in the Battle of the Somme.

remaining 2 months of fighting, the CEF was marked as a "shock force." A shock force is used mainly for breakthrough attacks. It must be a hard-fighting and determined group. The shock force leads an offensive, and it makes a break in the enemy line so that the rest of the army can pass through. While this was a great honour for the CEF, it was also the beginning of its career as the spearhead of countless Allied attacks.

Many lessons were learned during the Battle of the Somme. The Canadian commander of the First Division, Arthur Currie, questioned his front line troops about which techniques worked and which techniques did not work. He also talked to French soldiers. He used this information to train the Canadian army with new, more effective techniques.

Canadian artillery also made advancements in counter-battery fire in the period after the Battle of the Somme. With new scientific techniques for finding and destroying enemy guns, as well as a new organization and training system, the troops trained for their next challenge—attacking Vimy Ridge.

VIMY RIDGE

Vimy Ridge is known as the greatest battle in Canadian military history. Although it was only a small part of the Arras Offensive, and it was not followed by any other attacks, Vimy Ridge was a well-planned attack by the CEF. Using scientific methods, German guns were located in the sector. By the time of the attack, 83 percent of the German guns had been destroyed. Canadian engineers built long, underground communication systems and tunnels so they could not be cut by enemy guns. These tunnels also provided troops with a safe jump-off point from which to attack the enemy positions. At 5:30 a.m. on Easter morning, April 9, 1917, 15,000 CEF men climbed over the top of their trenches and attacked the German line at Vimy Ridge. Another 80,000 troops followed. Due to the accuracy of the artillery barrage, the first objectives of the battle fell quickly, and many German prisoners were captured. Many German troops were waiting underground for the barrage to end when Canadian troops attacked their trenches. After 5 days of fighting and 10,602 casualties, the CEF had taken 4 kilometres of enemy territory. The same location had cost the French army thousands of casualties. The location had remained uncaptured until the Canadians arrived. For his help in the attack, Arthur Currie was promoted to lieutenant-general and put in command of all Canadian troops. Vimy Ridge was the only successful attack of the entire Arras Offensive.

■ The determination of the Canadian Army at Vimy Ridge earned them a reputation as effective troops.

The CONSCRIPTION Crisis

Conscription cost Robert Borden any chance of being reelected prime minister.

From the beginning of World War I, Prime Minister Robert Borden knew it would be difficult to convince Quebec that **conscription** was necessary. It was difficult to portray the war as anything but a British war for British reasons. The Francophone people of Quebec did not want to participate in the war effort.

Canada tried to avoid using conscription. Instead, the government used the same tactics Great Britain used to convince men to voluntarily join the army—recruiting posters. These posters made statements such as "Your chums are fighting, why aren't you?"

Still, by 1917, not enough men were voluntarily enlisting as troops. Borden needed to maintain a strong army in the field so that the troops would be recognized as a Canadian army and not simply a colonial British army. In October 1917, Borden's term as prime minister was coming to an end, and he wanted to be reelected with a strong mandate. He changed the voting laws so that German Canadians could not vote. He also made it possible for women to vote on behalf of their husbands who were serving as soldiers overseas. In a speech in the House of Commons on May 18, 1917, Borden stated that "the time has come when the authority of the state should be invoked to provide reinforcements necessary to sustain the gallant men at the front who have held the line for months, who have proved themselves more than a match for the best troops that the enemy could send against them, and who are fighting in

FURTHER UNDERSTANDING

Prime Minister Robert Borden Robert Borden began his political career as a supporter of the British Empire. However, once he became prime minister, he realized it was necessary for Canada to hold an independent place within the British Empire. With the start of World War I and the loss of Canadian lives in Europe, Borden insisted on an independent voice for the nation with regard to international affairs. In 1915, Borden visited Canadian soldiers on the front lines and in hospitals in Great Britain. He demanded that Canada have more say in Allied planning.

The army was receiving fewer volunteers, so he proposed conscription. The issue of conscription divided the country and left Quebec with no representation in Borden's cabinet. In addition to dealing with the conscription crisis, Borden had to reorganize the country to meet the needs of a nation at war. At the end of the war, Borden insisted Canada have an independent delegation at the Paris Peace Conference. He also helped establish the League of Nations, which eventually became the United Nations (UN).

■ Sir Robert Borden was the eighth prime minister of Canada. He led the country between 1911 and 1920.

France and Belgium that Canada may live in the future." Borden officially proposed conscription with this speech and narrowly won the election. Since he won so few seats in the House of Commons, Borden formed a Unionist government. This government, which was a coalition with the Liberals who shared his view of conscription, held power between 1917 and 1920. Borden succeeded at enforcing conscription by the beginning of 1918, but it cost him any chance of being reelected prime minister.

In 1917, Borden was forced to put a stop to anti-conscription riots in Quebec City. It took decades for the people of Quebec to forgive the Conservative Party for instituting conscription.

"WHY DON'T THEY COME?"

WHY BE A MERE SPECTATOR HERE WHEN YOU SHOULD PLAY A MANS PART IN THE REAL GAME OVERSEAS?

JOIN THE 148TH Battalion.

A.A.MAGEE, LT COL.

Headquarters 197, PEEL ST. MONTREAL.

AFFILIATED WITH LL UNIVERSITY CONTINGENT NADIAN OFFICERS TRAINING CORPS.

The Canadian government used recruitment posters to convince young men to join the fight overseas.

The Path to VICTORY

The last German offensive of the war, Operation Michael, nearly succeeded in taking Amiens. If successful, this operation would not end the war, but it would put the Germans in a better bargaining position for peace negotiations. However, Operation Michael was not successful, and it left the German army weak. When the Canadians launched their attack alongside the Australians, it was against a weakened German army.

Still, the attack was not easy. The Germans knew a great deal about defence. The Canadians proceeded with their typical, repetitive practice attacks under the command of Arthur Currie. His instructions were carried down to the lowest ranks of the army by a highly efficient communication system. The Canadian force maintained that every soldier must know when he was going into battle, who he was fighting beside, who he was fighting against, what his goal was, and when he would eat his next meal.

Toward the end of the war, the reputation of the Canadian Expeditionary Force (CEF) as shock troops enabled the Germans to predict where the Allies were likely to attack. Therefore, when the time came to prepare for the final assault on Germany, Canadian forces were secretly moved to the front of the line for an attack toward Cambrai.

Canadian troops began marching toward their objectives on the Amiens line on August 8, 1918. Behind the cover of hundreds of tanks and aircraft, the Australians, British, Canadians, and French marched with little resistance. By mid-morning, they had penetrated 12 kilometres into German-held territory. The Germans called this their "black day" of World War I. Over the last 100 days of World War I, Canadian soldiers took more prisoners and land, and suffered fewer casualties than the American Expeditionary Force. The Armistice was signed and hostilities ended on November 11, 1918.

FURTHER UNDERSTANDING

Operation Michael Operation Michael was the last German offensive of World War I. The aim of this operation was to divide the French and British forces, and weaken them to the point that a counterattack was impossible. Although the Germans did not expect to win the war, the German high command thought that if this operation was successful, it would put them on equal footing with the Allied countries when peace negotiations started.

■ Following the battle of Amiens, Canadian soldiers advanced on foot to attack Cambrai.

THE HEROES OF THE CANADIAN EXPEDITIONARY FORCE

Billy Bishop

Baron von Richtoffen, the Red Baron, leads the list of World War I "air aces" with 80 confirmed kills. He is followed closely by Rene Fonck of France, who had 75 air victories. The third greatest air ace of World War I was Canadian William (Billy) Bishop, who had 72 confirmed victories. Bishop, who was the British Empire's top fighter pilot, had a tendency to crash his plane upon landing, but by the end of the war, he was a celebrated fighter ace. Of the top six fighter pilots flying for Great Britain during the war, four were Canadian. In addition to Bishop were Raymond Collishaw (60 victories), Donald Maclaren (54 victories), and William Barker (50 victories). Unlike many other pilots, Bishop survived the war. He lived until 1956.

■ Billy Bishop entered the Royal Military College in 1911, and was shipped overseas in 1915. He received the Military Cross for his actions at Vimy Ridge.

Arthur Currie

Arthur Currie was commander of the Canadian First Division and, later, the entire Canadian contingent in France. Before the war, he had worked as a businessperson, an insurance salesperson, and a schoolteacher. When the war began, he enlisted in the militia and worked his way through the ranks to become a lieutenant colonel of the artillery. Although he was not a professional soldier, he had a deep interest in his troops' health and safety, and a strong belief in preparation and training. His concern not only saved many Canadian lives, but also helped the Canadian forces achieve many victories. His training and attention to detail were two of the main reasons for Canada's success at Vimy Ridge in April 1917. He was an intelligent commander who was always willing to learn from the experiences of his troops and the troops of other nations. He remains one of Canada's greatest military commanders.

Francis Pegahmagabow

Francis Pegahmagabow was the son of the Chief of the Parry Island Band of the Ojibwa Nation. He enlisted in the Canadian army at the beginning of the war and served until it ended. Even though he was shot in the leg at Ypres, he returned to fight. His actions in battle earned him the Military Medal with two bars—meaning he earned the same medal three times. Many Canadian Native Peoples served with distinction in the CEF. Pegahmagabow became Chief of the Parry Island Band of the Ojibwa Nation. He lived until 1952.

WWI Summary Time Line

June 28, 1914

Archduke Francis Ferdinand is assassinated. Austria-Hungary declares war on Serbia and invades the next day.

August 1–12, 1914

All major European powers declare war on one another. Germany invades Belgium, and on August 4, Great Britain enters the war on the side of France and Russia. German troops move to France. Russian troops march to Germany, and on August 12, Great Britain and France declare war on Austria-Hungary. As a member of the British Empire, Canada is officially at war.

October 1, 1914

The first division of Canadian troops sails to Great Britain. The troops train for several months before entering the war on February 11, 1915.

February 11, 1915

The first Canadian soldiers land in France. They move directly to the northeastern section of the Ypres salient and fight alongside French-Algerian troops.

April 22–May 25, 1915

The Second Battle of Ypres occurs. Chlorine gas attacks cause a break in the Allied line between the French Algerians and the Canadians. The French Algerians fall back, and strong Canadian counterattacks help protect the line from German troops.

February 21, 1916

The Battle of Verdun, which is a German attempt to use the strategy of attrition on the French, begins. This disrupts planning for a massive French and British attack on the Somme, and the British are forced to attack with limited help.

July 1–November 18, 1916

The Battle of the Somme begins. The First Newfoundland Regiment is involved on the first day and sustains many casualties. The CEF enters the battle on September 15 with a new weapon—tanks. The first day of the Battle of the Somme is the worst day in the British army's history.

April 6, 1917

The United States declares war on Germany. After three years of selling weapons to both sides, the U.S. army chooses to fight on the side of Great Britain and Canada. United States troops begin to arrive in June 1917, but they do not fight until 1918, when the war is almost over.

April 9–May 4, 1917

The Battle of Arras, which includes the Canadian action at Vimy Ridge, begins. All Arras attacks fail except for the Canadian attack at Vimy Ridge.

December 5, 1917

Russia signs an armistice agreement with Germany. The armistice's terms included 30-day peace agreement and immediate peace negotiations. Germany focuses on battles in western Europe.

March 21, 1918
Germany launches a huge offensive at the Somme and makes enormous gains. This offensive is called Operation Michael. In April, they attack at Ypres, and in May, they attack on the Aisne. The Germans plan to attack with extra troops from the eastern front before U.S. troops enter the war. They almost succeed in taking the strategically important area of Amiens, but the offensive is unsuccessful.

September 26, 1918
The Allies make one final push to force Germany to surrender. Many call this action the "Last 100 Days."

November 1918
On November 3, Austria-Hungary signs an armistice agreement; Germany signs on November 11, and the war is over. Today, November 11 is celebrated in Canada as Remembrance Day.

■ The Canadian Memorial at Vimy Ridge opened in 1936. The names of 11,285 Canadian soldiers who died in France during World War I are engraved on the monument's walls.

After the War: TROUBLE at Home

Under the leadership of Prime Minister Borden, Canada signed the Treaty of Versailles as a separate nation from Great Britain. More than 65,000 Canadian men died for the British Empire in World War I. Their sacrifice helped liberate occupied France. It also began the process of Canada gaining independence from the British Empire. After the war, Canada became an **independent dominion**.

The conscription crisis, combined with other problems at the end of World War I, troubled Canadians. Although Borden won another term in office in 1917, his time as prime minister was coming to an end. The Conservative government fell into disorder, and by 1919 it had many problems to deal with.

One of these problems was the Influenza Epidemic of 1918–1919. Although 8,556,315 people died in World War I, it is estimated that the influenza outbreak killed between 20 and 40 million people worldwide. Fewer people died of the Black Death in 4 years than died of influenza in 1 year.

Approximately 40,000 Canadians died during the influenza epidemic. This epidemic prompted the federal government to create the Department of Health, which began co-ordinating Canada's health programs at a national level.

Another problem facing the government was the desire of many women to remain in the work force. After the war, men expected to return to work, but many women did not want to stop working. Magazine and newspaper articles begged women to return to their traditional roles as housekeepers and teachers. Magazine articles urged women to quit work and return home. Many women did return home, and the status of women in the workplace did not change for many years. Women were now able to vote, but for the most part, they were no longer allowed in the workplace.

FURTHER UNDERSTANDING

Co-operative Commonwealth Federation (CCF) The CCF was founded in 1932 by a number of socialist, farm, and labour groups that wanted to create a society in which every person would co-operate for the common good. The CCF was critical of **capitalism**, which they believed encouraged inequality, selfishness, and greed. In Regina in 1933, the CCF chose its first leader—J. S. Woodsworth, a Labour Member of Parliament from Winnipeg. The CCF also adopted the Regina Manifesto, which called for public ownership of key industries and social welfare programs for social services such as pension, medicare, family allowance, and unemployment insurance. The aim of the CCF was the elimination of capitalism by democratic means.

Influenza Influenza is a contagious disease caused by a virus in humans and in some animals. It is characterized by inflammation of the respiratory tract, irritation of the stomach, and fever. Influenza is commonly called the flu.

■ People wore masks over their noses and mouths to protect themselves from the influenza virus during the 1918–1919 outbreak.

Labour unrest was another problem facing Canada at the end of World War I. On May 15, 1919, there was a general strike in western Canada. The strike began in Winnipeg and immediately received worldwide attention. In New York and Great Britain, the issue received front-page newspaper coverage. A *New York Times* headline read "**Bolshevism** Invades Canada."

The workers at Vulcan Iron Works, Manitoba Bridge and Iron, and Dominion Bridge and Iron went on strike when their managers refused **collective bargaining**. In support, the building trades went on strike.

The government of Canada moved to prevent the spread of the strike. Justice Minister Arthur Meighen authorized the army to end the strike on June 17. Mass riots occurred when the strike ringleaders were arrested on June 21. Charles F. Gray, the mayor of Winnipeg, called in the army and the Royal Canadian Mounted Police (RCMP). In the confusion, the RCMP fired a shot into the crowd. One man was killed, and an unknown number of others were wounded. The strike was over.

The strike affected on Canadian labour. For example, in 1932, the Co-operative Commonwealth Federation (CCF) was established by original members of the strike. In 1961, the CCF and the Canadian Labour Congress combined to form the New Democratic Party. As well, William Lyon Mackenzie King, who was working for the Rockefeller Foundation in 1919, learned about the labour movement. When he joined the Liberal Party, he was able to change Liberal policy so that it addressed some of the workers' concerns.

■ On June 21, 1919, an organized protest became a riot on the streets of Winnipeg, Manitoba. This day is known as Bloody Saturday.

The ROARING Twenties

Canada entered the 1920s in a state of economic depression and with an enormous national debt. Unemployment was high, sometimes reaching 17 percent. Drought in the western provinces during 1917 and 1922 decreased Canadian wheat exports. In the early part of the twentieth century, wheat was Canada's single most important export. Still, after the influenza epidemic and the 1919 general strike, Canada finally started to recover from its economic slump. The twenties were a time of widespread investment, and the stock market was very popular.

By 1923, it was clear that the United States was Canada's primary trading partner. Without Great Britain's permission, Prime Minister William Lyon Mackenzie King signed Canada's first treaty with the United States—the Convention for the Preservation of the Halibut Fishery of the Northern Pacific Ocean. In 1926, Mackenzie King convinced Great Britain to declare Canada an independent member of the British Commonwealth.

In 1929, Canadian women were recognized as persons under the law. Five Alberta women, who became known as the "Famous Five," took the issue of women's rights to the Supreme Court of Canada. They wanted to have the word "persons" defined in the constitution to include women and not just men. This was known as the Persons Case. The Supreme Court ruled against the women, but when they took their case to Great Britain in 1929, the decision was reversed. In 1921, Agnes Macphail was elected Canada's first female Member of Parliament. In 1930, MacKenzie King appointed Cairine Wilson as Canada's first female senator.

During the 1920s, women were seeking liberation not only in politics but also in fashion. Shorter skirts and showing more skin became a popular trend in women's fashions. Young women called

FURTHER UNDERSTANDING

The Famous Five The Persons Case is one of the most famous cases in Canadian legal history. Five Alberta women—Henrietta Muir Edwards, Nellie McClung, Louise McKinney, Emily Murphy, and Irene Parlby—brought the case to the Supreme Court of Canada. These women, who became known as the Famous Five, asked the Supreme Court of Canada to declare that women were persons under the British North America Act and, as a result, that they were eligible to be appointed to the Senate.

The judges did not agree that women were persons under the Act. After speaking with several lawyers, and with the support of the government of Alberta and the prime minister, the five women appealed to the British Privy Council, which at that time was Canada's highest court of appeal. On October 18, 1929, the Privy Council declared that women were indeed persons. Today, Canadians celebrate "Person's Day," and since 1979, several women each year are awarded Person's Day medals.

■ In the 1920s, flappers rebelled against their parents' fashions. They wore clothes that showed more of their bodies and cut their hair into a short, "bob" style.

"flappers" wore baggy, comfortable skirts, and cut their hair short.

The 1920s were also known as the "prohibition years" because all of the provinces prohibited the sale of alcohol. This ban simply covered the sale of alcohol from public view. As a result, some people made their own alcohol or acquired a medical prescription so they could legally purchase alcohol. Some doctors believed that alcohol was a type of medicine. One doctor in Manitoba prescribed alcohol for 5,800 patients in 1 month.

Many Canadians invested large sums of money in the stock market, and many people kept their savings in stocks. For much of the 1920s, it was considered a good idea to invest in the stock market. Stocks continually increased in value. Not knowing whether to buy, sell, or hold, many people simply bought more shares. Radio stocks became the new, popular item and were being sold at high prices. On October 29, 1929, investment stopped. There were more stocks in supply than were demanded by investors. The price of shares

decreased, and people panicked. They sold every stock they had, and since nobody wanted to buy shares, their value dropped. This was one of the worst financial disasters in history. Thousands of people lost their life savings. Others who had taken loans to buy stocks not only lost their investment, but they also had debts to repay.

■ The Women's Christian Temperance Union was in favour of prohibition. It supported advertisements that deterred people from consuming alcohol.

Behind the Green Curtains

"Please Mother don't go in there..."

The Great DEPRESSION

Droughts in North America during the 1930s worsened the effect of the 1929 stock market crash. Unemployment was common, and low rainfall prevented many farmers in the United States and Canada from reaping healthy crops.

Canada was one of the countries that suffered most during the Great Depression of the 1930s. Since the main products in Canada were agricultural, the droughts of the 1930s had an adverse effect on wheat exports. Without these exports, large numbers of people living in the prairie provinces needed government assistance—at one point, 66 percent of the people in Saskatchewan were receiving help from the government. World trade also collapsed, and wheat prices fell. Canadian farmers were barely able to cover the cost of production, and many found it difficult to repay debts.

Pests such as gophers and grasshoppers also destroyed farmers' crops. In some places, grasshoppers were so numerous that it became too slippery to walk on the roads. Gophers became such pests that money was paid for gopher tails. For many people, hunting gophers was the only way to earn a living.

Ontario and Quebec had serious unemployment because mining and forest exports decreased. Despite this decrease, Ontario and Quebec were less affected by the depression than the West. The East's diversified industrial economies protected their domestic markets.

In British Columbia, the fish, lumber, and fruit markets were depressed, but they did not decrease as much as the agricultural markets in other provinces. The Maritime provinces had been in economic decline since the 1920s, so they were not as affected by the economic

FURTHER UNDERSTANDING

Communism Communism is a political and economic system that became one of the most powerful forces in the world. It shaped much of the world's history from the early 1900s to the 1990s. Some people have considered communism a threat to world peace. Others have seen it as the world's greatest hope. The goal of communism is to create a society that provides equality and economic security for all. In a communist system, land, factories, and other economic resources are owned by the government.

Democracy Democracy is a form of government that is ruled by the people. Democracy can either be direct or representative. Ancient Athens was a direct democracy, where the people voted on laws and other issues. Today, most democratic societies elect representatives to form a government that acts on behalf of the people. Most democratic societies value freedom and equality for their citizens. Three of the key freedoms of democracy are freedom of speech, freedom of the press, and freedom of religion.

In June 1935, Western Canadian workers, frustrated by increased unemployment, boarded eastbound trains to seek financial aid from the government. This is known as the On To Ottawa March.

depression. There was also a larger variety of jobs in the Maritimes, so they were not devastated by the failure of one market.

The Great Depression caused hard times throughout the world, and many countries fell into financial and political ruin. People looked to strong leaders to solve their problems. Brazil, Cuba, the Dominican Republic, El Salvador, Guatemala, Honduras, and Nicaragua all chose **dictatorship** over democracy.

In Canada, communists believed the nation's problems were caused by the rich, and only a revolution would fix the ailing economy. They believed the workers should rule and redistribute wealth and food by taking these items from those who had more and giving it to those in need. This form of government was practised in Russia.

Fascist movements were centred on powerful leaders such as Adolf Hitler in Germany, Benito Mussolini in Italy, and Juan Domingo Perón in Argentina. Fascist solutions involved a return to social and racial purity, a concentration of power in the central government, placing the state above the individual, and a return to a specific set of "virtues." Fascist leaders usually blamed their people's low economy on poor governing by former leaders.

Fascists in Canada believed that the depression should be blamed on immigrants and minorities. As in many other countries, Jewish citizens were a target of hatred. Adrian Arcand was the leader of the National Social Christian Party in 1934. He thought of himself as the "Hitler of Canada." His party wore red and white *swastika* armbands like the German Nazis. At the beginning of World War II, Arcand had planned to march to Ottawa and take over Canada, but he was arrested and put in a prison camp.

The Great Depression ended when the economy improved due to large sums of money spent in preparation for war against fascist governments.

■ Adrian Arcand, leader of the National Social Christian Party, was born in Quebec City, Quebec, in 1899.

■ Relief camps were created in 1935 for single, unemployed men. The camps were in poor condition, which led to protests. The camps paid men 20 cents per day for construction work.

State of the Nation on the Eve of **WAR**

Canada made an independent decision to enter World War II.

The League of Nations failed to stop the first hostile moves by Adolf Hitler and Benito Mussolini to expand their empires on the European continent and in Africa. Japanese attacks on China also occurred throughout the 1930s, but Canada had too many of its own problems to deal with outside conflict. Canada also reduced its military during the 1920s and 1930s. It did not have enough troops to send overseas. In 1939, on the eve of World War II, the Canadian army was almost nonexistent.

With the exception of fascist-dominated governments, countries around the world reduced their armies and talked about peace. On the eve of World War II, the Canadian Army had only 4,169 regular troops and 46,521 militia. The regular force was only large enough to defend small parts of Canada. The militia was poorly trained and had little equipment. It needed to be trained and reequipped

before it could contribute to the war effort. William Lyon Mackenzie King, reelected prime minister in 1935, had to find a way to rebuild the army when Germany invaded Poland.

Still, Canada declared war on Germany on September 10, 1939, 1 week after Great Britain. Canadians were enthusiastic about declaring war in 1914, but this was not the case in 1939. During World War I, almost every Canadian had a neighbour or loved one buried in a French or Belgian field. Even though Canadians did not look forward to another conflict in Europe, by the end of the first month of the war, 70,000 Canadians had joined the armed forces.

Although Mackenzie King was not completely in favour of taking Canada into another war, he knew that if Great Britain fell, Canada would face disaster. The Canadian economy depended on selling goods to Great Britain, but more

FURTHER UNDERSTANDING

Conscription Conscription, or compulsory military service, divided Canada in both World War I and World War II. When conscription was instituted during World War II, Prime Minister Mackenzie King promised that people forced to join the military would defend Canada and not be sent overseas. Since English Canada favoured conscription, Mackenzie King held a national vote asking the people of Canada to release the government from its promise not to send conscripted troops overseas. More than 72 percent of Quebeckers voted against conscription, while the rest of the country voted in favour. Still, Mackenzie King tried to prevent conscription, but by 1944, it became clear that conscription would be necessary. Twelve thousand conscripts were sent overseas.

The Rise and Fall of the League of Nations U.S. President Woodrow Wilson developed the basis for the League of Nations. He suggested creating a group of nations that would meet and discuss peaceful solutions to international problems. This plan

■ Canadians, including Prime Minister William Lyon Mackenzie King, voted in the plebiscite on conscription.

took shape in 1919 in the form of the League of Nations, which Canada joined as a founding member. A few problems emerged. The U.S., then the most powerful nation in the world and the least damaged after the war, did not join. It decided to avoid international politics. Germany and Russia were not allowed to join. Germany was being punished for its role in World War I, and Russia was excluded for its communist tendencies. The League failed to contain both Benito Mussolini and Adolf Hitler.

importantly, Canada was counting on the British navy to protect its vulnerable east coast.

At the beginning of the war, Canada sent materials to help Great Britain defend against Germany. Canada also prepared for potential war on its east coast. Halifax, Nova Scotia, became one of the world's most important seaports. Ships would leave carrying troops, guns, tanks, shells, foodstuffs, and other vital war materials. Ships would return carrying refugees, British children, German prisoners, and survivors of torpedoed boats.

Many Quebeckers supported Mackenzie King. Quebec refused to vote for the Conservative Party because Robert Borden had implemented conscription. On the eve of war with Germany, Mackenzie King dared not introduce conscription. Although most Canadians were in favour of helping Great Britain when it declared war on Germany on September 3, 1939, Mackenzie King was not as eager. He

eventually decided that Canada must help Great Britain. He waited long enough to make it clear that Canada was making an independent decision to enter the war.

In December 1939, Canada sent troops to Great Britain. About 61,500 young Canadian men enlisted to fight with Great Britain. To avoid conscription, Mackenzie King invested in an air force. Mackenzie King's thought that, fewer people died in the air force. That meant fewer replacement troops would be needed for Canada to remain an active part of the war effort. Canada's navy also gained many members. Before the war was over, about 350,000 men had joined the navy and the air force.

Women joined the Canadian Women's Army Corps (CWAC) as full-fledged soldiers, with rights to veteran's benefits. They performed the jobs of cooks and dispatch pilots, as well as hundreds of other important tasks throughout the Canadian services, both at home and overseas.

■ The British Commonwealth Air Training Plan was signed in December 1939. Many of the sites developed under this program became permanent Canadian Forces Bases.

The Rise of FASCISM in Germany

Adolf Hitler became chancellor of Germany in January 1933.

Adolf Hitler came to power in Germany in 1933. Before Hitler gained power, communists and fascists had been fighting for control of Germany.

Hitler had tried once before to gain control of Germany. Hitler and the National Socialist Party plotted to kidnap the leaders of the Bavarian government and force them at gunpoint to accept Hitler as their leader. Then, with the aid of World War I General Erich Ludendorff, they would win over the German army, proclaim a nationwide revolt, and bring down the German democratic government in Berlin. On November 8, 1923, Hitler and his party took the three highest-ranking officials of the German state of Bavaria hostage in a Munich beer hall.

The plan, known as the Beer Hall *Putsch*, failed, and Hitler was tried for treason. Hitler admitted his guilt in court. He could have received a life prison sentence, but the judges sentenced him to five years in jail. He would be eligible for parole after serving six months.

After Hitler's failed Beer Hall Putsch, Germany had signed agreements securing its borders against French and Belgian attacks. Germany also joined the League of Nations in 1926. The country was doing well until the 1929 stock market crash. Germany's economy declined, and hyperinflation took hold. Millions of Germans became unemployed. Germany was hit hard by the Great Depression. In this time of economic disaster, the communists and fascists fought for control of Germany.

During the 9 months Hitler spent in prison, he wrote the book, *Mein Kampf* (*My Struggle*), which is part autobiography

■ Hitler hoped to conquer the world. For a brief period of time, he controlled most of Europe and much of North Africa.

FURTHER UNDERSTANDING

Germany's hyperinflation

After World War I, Germany's economy was in ruins. The Treaty of Versailles forced Germany to make **reparation payments** to France. Germans called the Treaty a *Diktat* because they did not have any choice in its terms. It was dictated to them, and they were forced to sign. In 1914, the German mark was worth one quarter of a United States dollar. The failure of the German economy forced Germany into a spiralling inflation that put the value of the German mark at around $0.000000001 U.S. by October 1923. This was called hyperinflation because it was such large-scale inflation. Foreign governments intervened and brought the situation under control. Foreign financial intervention helped the national situation. This stability lasted until the Great Depression hit Germany.

and part political theory. When he left prison, he had a new plan. Instead of trying to take the country by force, he started a valid political party. He appointed a man named Josef Goebbels to be his party **propaganda** organizer. Hitler also made party organizations for women and children, which he believed would ensure the long-term future of his party. His party was called the National Socialists, or "Nazis." He ran for election in 1928, and won twelve seats in the government.

Hitler became chancellor of Germany in January 1933. He later formed a coalition government to take control of the nation. In 1933, Hitler passed the Enabling Act, which gave him total control over German affairs for 4 years. He used this time to remove unions and all political parties other than the Nazis.

In November 1933, Hitler called an election. With only one party in the race, Germany was firmly under Nazi control. Hitler completed his quest for power on the Night of the Long Knives, June 30, 1934. Hitler had all his rivals and major enemies killed. He killed about 400 members of his own party as well as others. In August 1934, President Hindenberg died. Hitler then combined the office of chancellor and president. He called himself *Fuhrer*.

Hitler had been a soldier in the German army during World War I. He believed the German army had not been defeated by the Allies. He decided that Germany had been betrayed from within. Jewish people were one of the main groups Hitler blamed for this betrayal.

Hitler believed Germany lost World War I because Jewish people had bankrupted the country, making it impossible for Germany to fight. Hitler used the idea of German nationalism and the public's distrust of Jewish people and communists to gain total control of Germany. Six million Jewish people were killed during World War II.

Kristallnacht, or the Night of Broken Glass, took place November 9 and 10, 1938. During Kristallnacht, Nazis terrorized people of German-Jewish descent. Many Jewish homes and businesses were destroyed.

Canada Joins the FIGHT

The German invasion of Poland, which caused Great Britain and Canada to declare war on Germany, did not immediately result in armed conflict. Although there were some British troops in France, fighting did not begin until May 1940. German war theorist Heinz Guderian used a mobile technique called *blitzkrieg* to overrun French defences and bypass the Maginot Line. The attack began on May 10, 1940, in Holland and Belgium. His techniques were so effective that by June 14, he was already marching his troops into Paris.

Allied forces, which consisted of troops from France and Great Britain, had retreated back to Dunkirk, France. On May 28, they left for England. By June 4, more than 300,000 British and French troops had been evacuated from Belgium.

Canadian troops had landed in northern France to assist the French troops, but the blitzkrieg happened too fast. Canadian troops arrived in Port of Brest, France,

between June 12 and 14. Late on June 14, Canadian troops evacuated back to England.

Canada's first action during World War II was in Hong Kong. The Japanese attacked Hong Kong on December 8, 1941, and the Canadians surrendered on Christmas day. During the battle, 1,975 Canadian soldiers were killed or taken prisoner by the Japanese. For the remainder of the war, prisoners were kept in terrible conditions. They were used as slave labourers in Japanese mines. Only about 1,400 troops returned home from Japan after the war.

FURTHER UNDERSTANDING

Blitzkrieg Blitzkrieg is a German word that means "lightning war." It was developed using British and French ideas about tank warfare after World War I. Heinz Guderian wrote the military classic *Achtung-Panzer!,* which talked about how to use tanks in battle. He theorized that tanks should have close assistance from dive-bombers and special infantry units to weaken the enemy and then use their armour and speed to break through the enemy line. This technique was very effective.

Maginot Line The Maginot Line was a long line of strong underground and above-ground defences that the French built along their border with Germany. It would have been very difficult for Germany to get through the Maginot Line. Instead, the German armies went around the line and captured Paris.

■ Propaganda, which is art used to communicate a message, was used to persuade the public to support World War II.

THE TORCH; BE YOURS TO HOLD IT HIGH! IF YE BREAK FAITH WITH US WHO DIE WE SHALL NOT SLEEP, THOUGH POPPIES GROW IN FLANDERS FIELDS.

McCREA.

Canadians asked to be included in the force that made the first attacks on Germany. Under the command of General Harry Crerar, Canadian troops took part in the raid at Dieppe on the north coast of France. The operation was cancelled once, but the raid on Dieppe finally occurred on August 19, 1942. The raid on Dieppe failed because the German defences were too strong. Tanks were unable to move through the soft sand or to climb the high cement walls that lined the beach. Of the 5,000 Canadian troops who participated in the raid, nearly 2,500 Canadian soldiers were wounded or captured.

Although the raid ended in disaster, British commanders thought it was a useful way of gathering information about German shore defences. Many Canadians at home were unhappy. They believed the British commanders used the Canadian soldiers as an experiment. Public opinion supported an attack on Europe, but Canadians were tired of hearing that their army was still training. Dieppe was a military disaster for Canada, and coming after the surrender of Canadian troops in Hong Kong, the morale of the Canadian army was very low.

■ Canadian troops travelled in landing crafts to meet up with British destroyers and prepare for the Dieppe Raid.

Canadian Troops in ITALY

Canadian troops were part of the Allied force that invaded Italy.

After a few devastating battles and years of training in England, Canadian soldiers were finally sent to the European continent. The Canadians were part of the Allied force that would invade Italy. Joseph Stalin, leader of the Soviet Union, asked the Allies to open a second front. This would take pressure off the Russian forces fighting German armies on the Russian Front in eastern Europe.

Winston Churchill, the prime minister of England, favoured attacking the Russian front. Churchill believed Allied troops could invade Italy more easily than they could invade France. On July 10, 1943, Canadian troops landed in Sicily and began a long, hard fight for Italy.

The First Canadian Tank Brigade and the First Canadian Division joined Bernard Montgomery's Eighth Army to invade Italy. Montgomery was well known in North Africa for defeating the Afrika Korps. After chasing the German and Italian forces through mountainous, hot Sicily, on July 15, 1943, the Canadians attacked Grammichele. They followed by taking the towns of Piazza Armenia and Valguanera. Canadian troops were involved in the battle for Sicily until August 7. Sicily was captured eleven days later. This was the first step toward defeating Germany

and its allies. Canadians captured about 250 kilometres of rocky, mountainous territory—more than any unit in the Eighth Army.

Canadian troops landed on the Italian mainland on September 3, 1943. They crossed the Straits of Messina and entered Italy through Reggio Calabria. Although the Canadian troops expected heavy resistance, they encountered almost none. Some Italian paratroopers put up a defence, but they were defeated by the Loyal Edmonton and the West Nova Scotia regiments. Italy surrendered on September 7, 1943. As the Germans retreated, they blew up bridges and destroyed anything that might be useful to the Allies.

On September 8, 1943, Allied forces landed at Salerno and battled against the German troops in southern Italy. Canadian troops rushed forward against very little

FURTHER UNDERSTANDING

The Russian Front Adolf Hitler had promised his generals that he would not force Germany to fight a two-front war. Many members of the German High Command felt that fighting on two fronts had caused Germany to lose World War I. Still, in the fall of 1940, Hitler ordered preparations for a massive attack to be launched on the Soviet Union the following spring. In 1941, the Germans attacked the Soviet Union with more than 3 million troops. Germany's war with the Soviet Union lasted until 1944. More than 27 million people were killed, and 25 million people were left homeless. The Soviet economy was devastated. Thousands of cities, towns, and villages were destroyed.

■ Winston Churchill was prime minister of Great Britain from 1940 to 1945, and 1951 to 1955. He was also a soldier, statesman, and journalist.

resistance. They covered about 500 kilometres before meeting strong German resistance. The German army tried to delay the Allies long enough to build a defensive line.

Canadian troops planned to cross a river and attack a city. Guns started their barrage, then the troops moved forward, and the city was captured. However, the Germans ran across the next river and destroy the bridges. This process was repeated until the Germans surrendered on May 2, 1945.

The Canadian forces in Italy became known as the **D-Day** Dodgers. These men did not fight

in D-Day because they were fighting in an area the D-Day troops believed was much easier territory than the north of France. The Canadian troops in Italy met very strong resistance, and their contribution to the war effort was just as important as the contribution of the troops who invaded France.

■ German soldiers surrendered to Canadian troops after the Canadians won the battle of Ortona.

ORTONA

By December 6, 1943, the Germans had fallen back as far as they had intended. They prepared to defend a town named Ortona on the Adriatic Coast of Italy.

The Germans prepared the city for a final stand. Everything, from doors to toilets, was booby trapped. The Germans planned to fight from the upper levels of houses. This made it difficult for the Canadians

to reach the Germans. In some instances, the Germans planted bombs in a house and waited until it was filled with Canadian soldiers before bombing the building. In one case, the Germans killed 19 Canadians using this technique. The streets were deadly, but Canadians soon learned a technique called "mouse holing." They would attack a house from bottom to top. Houses were usually

built in rows right beside each other, so the left wall of one house was the right wall of the next house. The Canadians would blow a hole in the wall at the top of one house and clear the next house from top to bottom.

The victory at Ortona came on December 27, 1943, at the cost of 2,339 dead and wounded Canadian soldiers.

WOMEN at War, Life at Home

The contribution of women was important to Canada's success in World War II.

Canadian women, who worked during World War I, joined the war effort in large numbers. Canadian Women's Army Corps (CWAC) troops were nurses, cooks, couriers, aircraft technicians, and pilots. Women worked in factories and hospitals, and built weapons. Women were not allowed to fight, but the services that women performed freed men to fight on the front lines. Although women who were not nurses were released from service at the end of the war, the Canadian army allowed women to join in 1951. In total, 21,624 women served in the CWAC. Before the end of the war, 146 women served in the war zone in northern Europe, and 43 served in Italy. Women served in 55 different military trades, and their contribution was very important to Canada's success in World War II.

Despite the war overseas, life in Canada continued as usual. Industries produced goods, such as weapons, to keep the Canadian army supplied. Single women were asked to replace their brothers in the workplace. Although they did the same jobs as men, they were paid much lower wages.

As the war continued, industry needed more workers. The government offered tax breaks and day-care services to draw married women into the work force. After the war, these benefits were removed. Many women returned to their traditional roles. In some cases, they were legislated back home. Many women did not leave the work force.

Clothing styles reflected the practical work women were doing during the war. Fussy, formal suits were kept in the closet for special occasions. Women wore casual clothing during the day. Long hair got in the way of factory machinery. Many women kept their hair tied back with scarves while they worked, or they cut their hair short. Women also wore short sleeves and work shirts.

Canadian productivity increased during the war. Many nations were unable to produce war equipment and supplies, so when Canada began producing goods, there was a large market for the products.

■ In 1942, the Canadian government began relocating Japanese nationals and Japanese Canadians to internment camps in British Columbia and Alberta.

FURTHER UNDERSTANDING

Internment camps During World War II, the Canadian government worried about spies and saboteurs. To prevent trouble on the home front, Canada sent 24,000 Japanese Canadians, including 7,400 naturalized Canadian citizens, to internment camps. Canada imprisoned 700 Italian Canadians in internment camps, and between 1939 and 1945, the Canadian government arrested and interned 837 German-Canadian farmers, workers, and club members who had been denounced or were considered disloyal. The Japanese-Canadian community received a settlement in 1988 to compensate for its internment and loss of property during World War II. They were offered a $12 million community development fund, along with $21,000 to every survivor of Canadian World War II internment camps.

Canada's agricultural products continued to be very important, but heavy industry became increasingly important to Canada's economy after the war.

Many believed the home front should be kept safe from people who were considered dangerous. The presence of communists, Germans, Italians, and Japanese people living in Canada worried the government. The government banned the Communist Party, and German, Italian, and Japanese Canadians were forced to move to internment camps. Many German Canadians were kept in southern Alberta and forced to work as farm labourers. After Pearl Harbor and Hong Kong, some Canadians were concerned about Japanese Canadians living in Canada. This fear turned to panic when a Japanese submarine was seen off the coast of Vancouver Island in 1942. During the war, about 24,000 Japanese Canadians were moved from their homes to places including Kelowna, British Columbia, and Lethbridge, Alberta. Their homes, businesses, and possessions were sold, and they were forced to begin new lives. The laws against Japanese Canadians were not lifted until 1947.

CANADA'S WARRIOR WOMEN

Jerry Mumford

Jerry Mumford was from a service corps in Halifax and was sent to Great Britain during 1940. She helped put out fires and assisted people with injuries while bombs fell on London. She was one of the few women selected to travel to Italy with the Canadian army in 1944. In Italy, Mumford worked, occasionally without sleep, to get wounded troops to safety.

Maude Elizabeth Steen

Maude Elizabeth Steen became a radio operator after training in Canada. Female radio operators were only allowed to travel to the war effort on ships from Norway. She made her way onto a Norwegian ship, the *S.S. Viggo Hansteen*. Ten weeks after she signed on board the ship, it was torpedoed by a German submarine. Steen lost her life helping deliver troops for the war effort.

■ The creation of the Canadian Women's Army Corps (CWAC) was a major accomplishment in the history of women's participation in the Canadian military. In total, about 3,000 women served overseas during World War II.

The Tide Turns: BARBAROSSA

Once Hitler had control of Western Europe, he turned his attention to the Soviet Union.

Adolf Hitler signed a non-aggression pact with Joseph Stalin, leader of the Soviet Union, before Germany attacked Poland. Hitler wanted to ensure that Germany's eastern flank was safe before it attacked the west. This was similar to Germany's World War I win-hold-win strategy. In this case, the East was not defended by troops, it was defended by the pact. Once Hitler had control of western Europe from Poland to the border of Spain, he turned his attention to the Soviet Union, ignoring the pact.

In his book, *Mein Kampf*, Hitler said that a war with the Soviet Union would strengthen the German people. First, they would take, and use, the Ukraine's grain-rich territory to feed their people. He called this idea *Lebensraum*, which means "living space." Once Germany was in control of the Ukraine, Germany would not have to worry about a British blockade starving the German population, which happened in World War I. Next, the eastern front would be a place of almost constant war, where his German youth would train in real combat against a race of people Hitler considered inferior. This attack was code named Operation Barbarossa, after a well-known German Crusades hero.

According to legend, in Germany's time of need Barbarossa the hero would rise from the dead and fight for Germany.

The German army advanced to the edge of Moscow, where they encountered many problems. German tanks did not perform well in the Russian winter, and the German army did not have proper winter clothing. It took more than 3 months for German forces to reach Moscow.

The Soviet army stopped the German forces before they reached Moscow. Once the German troops were stopped, Stalin ordered the Soviet army to attack. The German's failure to capture Moscow marked a turning point in World War II. The Soviet army's success was due in part to their equipment. The T-34 series tank

FURTHER UNDERSTANDING

Deep Doctrine, or Deep Battle The Deep Doctrine, or Deep Battle strategy employed by the Soviet army in World War II used a combination of scorched earth tactics, **guerrilla warfare** behind Nazi lines, and strategic retreats that protected reserves and sapped the enemy's strength. While Stalin did not want the army to retreat, when it became necessary, the Soviet army was expected to destroy anything that could be used by the German army. In addition, the Soviets dismantled and moved most of their factories far behind the battle lines. These tactics enabled the Soviet army to replenish the equipment it had lost during the early stages of Operation Barbarossa and regroup.

■ Joseph Stalin commanded Russia's armed forces after Germany attacked Russia in June 1941. Stalin held absolute power in the Soviet Union for nearly 25 years.

was fast, it worked well on snow and mud, and it had thick armour. More importantly, the Soviets had developed a form of blitzkrieg. It was called Deep Doctrine, or Deep Battle.

The winter of 1941 to 1942 was very cold, and the snow and mud made it difficult to move vehicles, including tanks.

The Germans' lack of winter clothing resulted in many casualties. This gave the Russians time to train more soldiers, build defences, and stop the German attacks. Throughout the winter months, the Soviet army mounted attacks on all fronts, beginning the push that forced the German army back to Germany.

■ In September 1944, Canadian troops attacked German soldiers defending Calais. Civilians were able to evacuate during a temporary truce in the fighting.

PREPARATION FOR INVASION

Italy was drawing troops away from the German attack on the Soviet Union, but not as many as the Allies wanted. The Allies planned to invade fortress Europe. In 1943, the Allies realized that they were not just fighting to rid the world of Hitler. If the Allies did not soon reach Berlin, Europe might become run by international communism. The Allies decided to invade France. Where to attack was a serious question for those people planning the invasion. Calais was located closest to England, and it would likely be where Hitler expected the invasion to occur. Instead, the Allies chose a stretch of beach between Caen and the Cotentin Peninsula. The Allies deceived the Germans into thinking Calais was the attack point. One of the tricks they used to deceive the Germans was to drop bombs on areas near Calais. Another was to send false radio signals from a phantom army in South England.

D-DAY: Juno Beach

Once the Canadian troops were united, they were able to liberate Holland.

By June 1944, the Allies were ready to invade France. On June 6, 1944, the Third Canadian Division and the Second Canadian Armoured Brigade landed in Normandy with more than 150,000 Allied troops. The area of the invasion was defended by cement walls, rotating motorized gun turrets, machine gun nests, and tank traps. Of the entire Allied force that landed on D-Day, only one unit—a troop of Canadians—achieved their objective. On the first day alone, 340 Canadians died, and another 574 were wounded taking the beach. Hitler expected the invasion to occur at Calais, and the German army was late moving troops to force the Allies off the beaches. Soon, the rest of the Canadian army in Great Britain crossed to the battlefields of France.

Operation Atlantic took the Canadians through Colombelles over the Orne River. The Canadians were on the far eastern side of the Allied line alongside the British army. The U.S. army was on the open side to the west. They encountered tough resistance. The Canadian and British armies held the Germans in order to give the U.S. army time to break out and get behind the German flank. The U.S. army postponed their breakout, and the Canadian army made many bloody attacks to keep the Germans in place. Finally, the U.S. army broke out and rushed to encircle the German forces.

A problem early in the Normandy campaign was to close the Falaise Gap. Since the Canadians were the farthest east on the line, they had to form part of the "gate" that would close around the German armies in northwest France. It was difficult for both the U.S. and the Canadian armies to close the gap. Thousands of German soldiers escaped every day, and the same German division that had fought the Canadians on D-Day came to help keep the gap open. The U.S. forces stopped at the city of Argentan, which meant Canadian troops would have to close the last few kilometres of the gap. They closed the gap on August 21, 1944.

FURTHER UNDERSTANDING

Battle of the Bulge By late 1944, it was clear that Germany was losing the war. The Soviet army was closing in on the eastern front, and German cities were being destroyed by intense U.S. bombing. The Italian peninsula had been liberated, and the Allied armies were advancing rapidly through France. Hitler needed to slow down the Allied advance. He decided to invade through the Ardenne Forest, where Germany had surprised France at the beginning of the war. The plan was to capture Antwerp, Belgium. Hitler hoped this would give Germany time to work on its secret weapons and train fresh troops. The plan failed and cost Germany most of its remaining air force. They lost approximately 100,000 troops, who were killed, wounded, or captured.

■ On June 6, 1944, Allied forces invaded western Europe along an 80-kilometre front in Normandy, France. Of the more than 150,000 Allied troops, 14,000 were Canadian. Canadians suffered 1,074 casualties during this battle.

Just after closing the Falaise Gap, Canadian forces in Italy made an important breakthrough at the Gothic Line. This breakthrough assisted the push through Italy. Still, the Canadian troops in Italy had quite a bit of fighting to do before they could join the rest of the Canadian army for the battle to secure the Scheldt River in Holland. Once the Canadian troops were united, they were able to liberate Holland.

During the Battle of the Bulge, also called the Ardennes Offensive, the Germans counterattacked and almost succeeded in knocking the Allied armies back. The offensive failed. The Canadian army moved into Germany on February 8, 1945.

THE SCHELDT

After successfully landing in France, Canadian troops were in position to move along the north coast of Europe toward the east. After some fighting, they made their way east to Belgium and the Scheldt River. The Canadians had to take the mouth of the Scheldt River, called an estuary, in order for the Allied attack to advance. This would allow river passage from the English Channel far inland. This was necessary to get supplies to the Allies. The task was difficult, and the Canadians were not well-equipped for the job.

However, the Canadian army succeeded in taking the Scheldt estuary, and went on to liberate Holland. The Dutch people still remember and celebrate Canada's sacrifice for their freedom.

■ Dutch people celebrated in the streets after Canada liberated Holland in 1945.

Changes in Canada and the WORLD

The atomic bombs dropped on Japan at the end of the war may have been a warning to the Soviet Union to stop at Berlin.

Victory in Europe came when the Allied and Soviet armies joined together in Germany. An end to the fighting was declared on "Victory in Europe Day," also known as VE Day, May 8, 1945. The Soviet Union had caused the most damage to Germany over the course of the war. Nine out of every ten German casualties were injured by Russian soldiers. When the Soviet Union and the Allies met in occupied Germany, the Cold War had already begun. The Soviet army was enormous, and some people were worried that it would not stop at Berlin, but might try to take over the rest of Europe. George Patton, a U.S. General, recommended that the western Allies attack Stalin and remove a dangerous dictator from the world before he became too strong. The atomic bombs dropped on Japan at the end of the war may have been a warning to the Soviet Union to stop in Berlin and not to try to take control of any other countries. Although the Soviet Union and the western nations did not go to war, the situation in Europe soon turned into a war of political beliefs. Communism confronted capitalism in the Cold War that lasted until the break-up of the Soviet Union in 1991.

After Japan's defeat later in the year, World War II was truly over. The Allies realized that the Treaty of Versailles was not a peace treaty, but a way of punishing Germany. Instead of imposing another punishing treaty on Germany, the western Allies began to rebuild the country. The Soviet Union, however, started looting their side of Germany. They stole industrial secrets, scientists, and factories. They wanted to use German advances to better their technology in the Soviet Union. An imaginary line called the "Iron Curtain" was drawn across Germany and across Europe. Many confrontations were yet to come between the Soviet Union and the western nations.

Many Canadians who lived in Great Britain during the first 4 years of the war married local women. After the war, the Canadian population exploded because of these "war brides." In 1946, 47,000

People across Canada celebrated Victory in Europe Day (VE-Day). The war affected Canadians of all ages.

FURTHER UNDERSTANDING

Cold War The Cold War between the U.S. and the Soviet Union lasted from 1945 to 1991. Although there was never any physical fighting, a war still occurred. In this case, the war was fought with words. The two most powerful nations, the U.S. and Soviet Union, were arguing about which type of government and society was the best. The U.S. has always been a democracy, with a strong capitalist base. A capitalist system is based on the belief that private citizens have the right to own businesses and earn money on their own merit. The Soviet Union was a communist society. A communist system is based on the idea that all factories and production are controlled by the government. The government then distributes the wealth evenly among its citizens so that poverty is eliminated.

European and British women and their 21,000 small children returned to Canada with their husbands.

The Canadian government provided the women and children with sea and rail transport so they could travel to Canada. They were even given food allowances and medical care. The Canadians were so popular with English women that an office was set up in London to offer advice about life in Canada. In 1947, the government declared that all people living in Canada were Canadian citizens. This included women from other countries who had just arrived as war brides. All Canadians had the same rights under the law.

Canada had already started to sever its ties with Great Britain before World War II. During and after the war, Canada's ties became stronger with the U.S. In 1938 and 1940, Canada and the U.S. signed agreements of mutual assistance in wartime. In 1957, the U.S. and Canada established the North American Aerospace Defence Command (NORAD) to defend North America from potential Soviet nuclear bombs. Canada and the U.S. now share the longest undefended border in the world.

■ War brides, such as Margery Clioby and her daughter Sandra, broke ties with their homes and families to begin a new life in Canada. The arrival of these women and their children in Canada marked the largest wave of immigration since the Great Depression.

WWII Summary Time Line

March 14, 1939
Germany takes over Czechoslovakia.

August 23, 1939
Germany and the Soviet Union sign the Molotov-Ribbentropp Pact, agreeing not to attack one another. This leaves Germany free to fortify Europe.

September 1, 1939
Germany attacks Poland. Soviet troops invade Poland from the east on September 17. Poland surrenders to Germany on September 27.

September 3, 1939
The British ship *Athenia* is sunk by German U-boats off the coast of Ireland. Great Britain and France declare war on Germany.

March 18, 1940
Italy allies with Germany against Great Britain and France.

May 10, 1940
Using the tactics of blitzkrieg, the German army travels through Holland and Belgium to France. Canadian troops land in France. They are removed as the conflict worsens. Paris is occupied on June 14.

June 22, 1941
German troops invade the Soviet Union, breaking the Molotov-Ribbentropp Pact.

December 7, 1941
Pearl Harbor is attacked by the Japanese. Japan also attacks the Philippines and Hong Kong. The U.S. is at war with Japan, and it declares war on Italy and Germany on December 11. Hong Kong is Canada's first major battle in the war, and all Canadian troops are either killed or taken prisoner.

August 19, 1942
The Dieppe raid is the Canadian troops' second major battle of the war. The Allied troops are not successful, and they retreat to Great Britain.

July 10, 1943
Allied troops invade Sicily, causing the fall of the Italian government only weeks later. Germans in Italy take over the country and prepare for an Allied attack. Canadians remain fighting in Italy until late 1944.

June 6, 1944
D-Day, the Allied invasion of Europe, takes place. At the time, this is the largest marine invasion in history. Canadians fight at Juno Beach, which was east of the main landing areas.

August 25, 1944
Paris is liberated.

December 16, 1944
The German Ardennes Offensive begins. It is also called the "Battle of the Bulge." U.S. soldiers fight to keep the Germans from Antwerp, Belgium.

May 7, 1945

Germany surrenders to the Allies. Germany is divided into two halves. One half is occupied by the western Allies, and the other half is occupied by the Soviet Union.

August 6, 1945

The U.S. launches the first nuclear attack in history on the Japanese city of Hiroshima. A second bomb is dropped on Nagasaki days later.

August 10, 1945

Japan surrenders to the United States.

■ Many of the Canadian soldiers who were killed in action on Juno Beach on D-Day are buried at the Beny-Sur-Mer Canadian War Memorial in Normandy.

QUIZ

(answers on page 47)

Multiple Choice

Choose the best answer in the multiple choice questions that follow.

1 Whose assassination in 1914 led to World War I?
a) Otto von Bismarck
b) Archduke Francis Ferdinand
c) First Sea Lord Winston Churchill
d) Czar Nicholas II

2 What does the acronym CEF stand for?
a) Canadian European Foundation
b) Canadian Emergency Force
c) Canadian Environmental Forestry
d) Canadian Expeditionary Force

3 What was the issue that divided French and English Canada during World War I?
a) communism
b) segregation
c) conscription
d) wheat exports

4 Canadians experienced one of their greatest victories in World War I during the attack at Amiens in 1917. What was the name of this battle?
a) Vichy
b) Verdun
c) Vickers
d) Vimy Ridge

5 Who was prime minister of Canada when World War II began?
a) William Lyon Mackenzie King
b) Robert Borden
c) Wilfrid Laurier
d) Arthur Meighen

6 Where was Canada's first battle in World War II, and who did they fight?
a) Pearl Harbor, Japanese
b) Dieppe, Germans
c) Normandy, Germans
d) Hong Kong, Japanese

7 What was the name of the gap that the Canadians had to close to surround the German army in 1944?
a) Caen
b) Falaise
c) Scheldt
d) Ortona

8 What country did Canadian troops liberate during, and after, the battles for control of the Scheldt River?
a) Holland
b) France
c) Luxembourg
d) Denmark

Mix and Match

Match the description in column A with the correct terms in column B. There are more terms than descriptions.

A

1) Prime Minister of Canada during World War I
2) Fuhrer of Germany in World War II
3) Emperor of Germany in World War I
4) Canadian flying ace in World War I
5) Commander of the First Canadian Division in World War I
6) Prime Minister of England during World War II
7) Leader of the Canadian Fascist Party

B

a) Arthur Currie
b) Adolf Hitler
c) Robert Borden
d) Billy Bishop
e) Wilhelm II
f) Georgi Zhukov
g) Adrian Arcand
h) Winston Churchill

Time Line

Find the appropriate spot on the time line for each event listed below.

A German troops invade the Soviet Union

B The Battle of the Somme

C D-Day: The invasion of Europe

D The U.S. launches the first nuclear attack in history

E Archduke Francis Ferdinand is assassinated

F Germany takes over Czechoslovakia

June 28, 1914 **1**
February 11, 1915 The first Canadian soldiers land in France
April 22–May 25, 1915 The Second Battle of Ypres
July 1–November 28, 1916 **2**
April 6, 1917 The U.S. declares war on Germany
April 9–May 4, 1917 The Battle of Arras
November 11, 1918 World War I ends

March 14, 1939 **3**
September 1, 1939 Germany attacks Poland
September 3, 1939 Great Britain and France declare war on Germany
June 22, 1941 **4**
August 19, 1941 Dieppe Raid
December 7, 1941 Pearl Harbor is attacked by the Japanese
July 9, 1943 The Allies invade Sicily
June 6, 1944 **5**

August 25, 1944 Paris is liberated
December 16, 1944 The German Ardennes Offensive begins
May 7, 1945 Germany surrenders
August 6, 1945 **6**
August 10, 1945 Japan surrenders

Conclusion

Over the course of 31 years and two world wars, Canada went from being a colony of Great Britain to a respected member of the world community. Canada's alliance and business ties slowly shifted from Great Britain to the U.S. In one generation, the British subjects of the colony of Canada became Canadian citizens in the Independent Dominion of Canada.

Prime Minister Robert Borden used Canada's involvement in World War I to help Canada gain independence from Great Britain. Canada's contribution to World War I allowed Canada to have a seat at the armistice talks. Canada also signed the Treaty of Versailles as a country separate from Great Britain. While full independence did not happen until the ratification of a new Canadian constitution in 1982, at the end of World War I, Canada had come a long way from being a British colony.

During World War I, Canadian women began the journey to gaining full equality in Canadian society. They were granted the right to vote and worked in non-traditional jobs. Between the two wars, women were declared persons in the eyes of the law. In World War II, Canadian women were allowed to join the armed forces in limited positions, and in the 1950s, they were allowed to join the army.

The Great Depression hurt the Canadian economy, and it was not until World War II that the country overcame its economic slump. The changes that started in World War I continued in World War II. Canada finally became an independent nation. For Canada, the turbulent years of the early twentieth century were an opportunity to create a new nation.

Further Information

Suggested Reading

Bercuson, David J. *Maple Leaf Against the Axis. Canada's Second World War.* Don Mills, ON: Stoddart, 1995.

Gossage, Carolyn. *Greatcoats and Glamour Boots: Canadian Women at War, 1939-1945.* Toronto: Dundurn Press, 2001.

Granatstein, Jack L. *Canada's Army: Waging War and Keeping the Peace.* Toronto: University of Toronto Press, 2002.

Lambert, Barbara Ann. *Rusty Nails and Ration Books: Memories of the Great Depression and World War II, 1929-1945.* Victoria, BC: Trafford, 2002.

Internet Resources

Canada: A People's History Online
history.cbc.ca
The online companion to CBC's award-winning television series on the history of Canada, as told through the eyes of its people. This multimedia Web site features behind-the-scenes information, games and puzzles, and discussion boards. The site is also available in French.

The Canadian Encyclopedia Online
www.thecanadianencyclopedia.com
This is an excellent reference site for all things Canadian. In-depth history articles are accompanied by photographs, paintings, and maps. Articles can be accessed in both French and English.

Glossary

attrition: a gradual wearing down

autonomy: self-government

balance of power: when nations make alliances against one another so that no one nation is stronger than another

Bolshevism: communism

capitalism: a system of government that allows private citizens to own companies and compete for profit

chancellor: head of German government

collective bargaining: when workers band together to bargain for their salaries and rights

conscription: required enrolment in military service

D-Day: June 6, 1944; the day the Allies invaded Normandy, France

dictatorship: a government with no competing parties

fascist: advocating a one-party political system based on a powerful leader and extreme pride in one's country and race

Great Powers: the strongest nations in Europe before World War I

guerrilla warfare: war fought by small bands of fighters that attack the enemy with surprise raids and bombings

howitzer: a short cannon that fires shells in a high curve

Independent Dominion: Canada's self-governing status as a member of the British empire

militia: part-time military

outflank: to wrap an army force around the edge of the enemy's army force

propaganda: signs and posters used to spread opinions and beliefs

regiment: an organization of soldiers that has a name and comes from a specific area

reparation payments: money that a defeated nation is forced to pay to conquering nations

salient: a portion of a fort or a line that extends into enemy territory

xenophobic: an abnormal fear or hatred of foreign peoples

Answers

Multiple Choice	Mix and Match	Time Line
1. b)	1. c)	1. e)
2. d)	2. b)	2. b)
3. c)	3. e)	3. f)
4. d)	4. d)	4. a)
5. a)	5. a)	5. c)
6. d)	6. h)	6. d)
7. b)	7. g)	
8. a)		

Index